Spelling Recovery

/ˈspelɪŋ/ /rɪˈkʌvəri/

Jan Roberts

 David Fulton Publishers

First published 2001
by The Australian Council for Educational Research Ltd
19 Prospect Hill Road, Camberwell, Victoria, 3124

Published in Great Britain (with amendments) by
David Fulton Publishers, 414 Chiswick High Road, London W4 5TF

10 9 8 7 6 5 4 3 2 1

British Library Cataloguing-in-Publication data
A catalogue record for this book is available from the British Library

ISBN 1 84312 192 1

Printed in Great Britain

Contents

Foreword

Many years ago Russell Stauffer wrote a useful and influential book entitled *Teaching Reading as a Thinking Process*. Now Jan Roberts, in *Spelling Recovery*, has written an extremely useful book that could easily have been subtitled *Teaching Spelling as a Thinking Process*. She frequently reminds teachers of the need to discuss with their students the 'why' and the 'how' of learning to spell words and carry out corrections. While recognising the role of direct teaching, repetition, and practice to achieve automaticity in spelling, Jan's approach to instruction stresses meaningful learning rather than mere rote memorisation.

In *Spelling Recovery*, Jan Roberts has provided teachers with a wide variety of methods for helping children become interested in words and confident in their own ability to learn even the trickiest of spelling patterns. The starting point for building a child's skills and confidence in spelling is always to identify what he or she already knows, and what he or she can almost achieve unaided. Jan's diagnostic procedures will help teachers obtain this information quickly and efficiently. The forms of instruction (scaffolding) she then recommends are geared to each student's needs.

The teaching approaches illustrated in *Spelling Recovery* reflect Jan's years of teaching experience: they are student-centred and fun, yet embody the appropriate degree of structure to ensure maximum progress. I love her advice, 'Keep the lesson moving. Students get restless if you are too slow or if you talk for more than a minute without engaging them in response.' Many studies have found that the pace of instruction is an important variable influencing children's learning, with the most impressive results occurring in programmes where the pace is quite fast and with many opportunities for children to respond. The approaches described in *Spelling Recovery* facilitate both pace and participation.

Jan states, 'Thorough, enthusiastic, interesting and challenging teaching is the key to improving your students' spelling.' I couldn't agree more; and this book will help teachers (and parents) to implement such teaching. It is always essential to remember, however, that accurate spelling should never be seen as an end in itself. Proficient, automatic spelling is important simply because it frees up cognitive capacity and effort so that a writer's attention can be devoted fully to generating ideas and expressing these clearly. Jan would be the first to agree that the efficacy of any spelling programme must be judged by the extent to which its principles and content transfer and generalise to children's every-day writing. Teaching to ensure transfer is a vitally important issue that you, the reader, must address as you apply the practical advice from this book to improve the spelling ability of your own students.

Peter Westwood
University of Hong Kong

Introduction

In every classroom there are students with different spelling abilities. As an educator, you need to be aware of the causes of spelling problems, and what appropriate action can be taken to help these students become competent spellers. An extra advantage of improving spelling is the flow-on effect to students' reading and writing skills. Increasing their decoding capacity 'frees' students to concentrate on the task of reading comprehension; and knowing how to spell improves quality and speed in writing.

Approximately 5-10 per cent of all students experience learning difficulties with language. The severe form of this is called 'specific learning disability' (and 'dyslexia' by the Department of Education and Employment).[1] These students often experience a range of spelling errors that can overwhelm them and their teachers.

However, spelling errors and their causes can be analysed and appropriate action designed and implemented by teachers and students. Current research and the author's personal experience indicate that most students, especially those with learning difficulties, benefit from SISS teaching, that is *s*pecific, *i*nteresting, *s*tructured and *s*trategic. This book addresses the ways you can achieve this and has been designed to be used in two ways:

1 When you identify an occasional error being made by a particular student, or a common error made by several students in your class, you can locate this type of error in the book and implement specific action.
2 To help students with pronounced, multiple spelling problems, an analysis of their spelling is recommended first (see Appendix 1, Spelling Error Analysis Record). Then you decide on a priority of learning outcomes (goals) and select appropriate action to implement.

Why teachers need to take action

As long as spelling is regarded as important, teachers have a responsibility to take action. Every time a word is written incorrectly, the writing hand practises and learns the error. How often have you seen a student write 'because' as 'becose'? The student may know it is wrong but has learnt the error too thoroughly. Changing a learned pattern is harder than remembering new learning, so a balance must be struck between supporting the creative process through 'free' writing and preventing the learning of incorrect spelling.

Students who make frequent spelling errors hate feeling 'stupid' so avoid asking for help, write as little as possible or meander with 'safe' words. Students need support to learn how to spell the words most frequently written, to know how to spell 'new' words, to understand how to use references and to approach their errors more positively, so that they can concentrate on the important content and structure of their writing.

Teaching approaches

Systematic teaching

To overcome spelling problems as quickly as possible, teachers need to be specific in their teaching approach. This means that, as the facilitator in the learning process, you need to appreciate the cause of the problem, decide on the specific learning outcome you want to achieve, implement appropriate action and assess its success. This requires you to be clear about the learning goals. In a direct teaching approach, you should tell students, as simply as possible, what they need to know and how this can be achieved.

Students (especially those with learning difficulties) benefit from programmes that combine direct teaching with student-centred learning.[2] Students who make frequent errors will benefit from direct teaching of the essentials, especially high frequency words and the 'demon words' (those most commonly misspelt, see Appendix 7). This approach includes incidental teaching within other reading and writing activities. It is important for students to see spelling as part of all literacy. Addressing errors as they occur is a meaningful way to show this to students.

However, current research indicates that you cannot rely on incidental learning to teach students with special needs. Such students do not generalise this learning without direction and practice.

Repetition

An important structural element of learning spelling is repetition. Students with efficient cognitive processing do not need external help – they provide their own mental repetition. But the majority of students need more repetition than is often provided. Games provide an incentive for students to concentrate on repetition of the same learning and provide one of the fastest ways to strengthen students' learning of spelling. Students regard any activity in which participants take turns as a game. It is quite simple to adapt traditional word games that require the players to spell, explain a rule, or demonstrate the use of a word. For example, Noughts and Crosses and Battleships are effective games that require only paper and pen. Snap, using cards you can make yourself, is a powerful way to learn vowels, consonants and letter patterns.

Teaching 'how to' strategies

Many students, especially those with learning difficulties, have no conscious strategies at all, and they often assume that everyone else 'just knows' the answer. You can help students by teaching deliberate, step-by-step, metacognitive strategies. Teachers need to develop skills in teaching 'how to' strategies, so that the students can understand the thinking process behind correct spelling.[3] Spelling is a thinking process, not a rote-learning one.[4] You may need to teach students how to tackle the spelling of a 'new' word (see Appendix 3); and how to memorise the spelling of frequently used words. The 'look, cover and write' process works for many children, however, the CHIMP strategy developed by the author is more effective (see Appendix 2).

Strategies can include memory tricks and 'talking through' the strategy. Here is an example of a student using a metacognitive strategy to decide whether or not to double a consonant:

Lucy: How many 'p's' will I put in 'shopping'? I'm adding an ending so I have to listen to the vowel before the 'p'. That's 'o'. It's not saying its name so it must be a short vowel. So it needs two consonants. I'll write: 's h o p p i n g'.

Commercial spelling programmes

There are several structured spelling programmes available that introduce learning systematically and provide excellent practice activities.[5] You may need to select appropriate sections and you will need to introduce each topic thoroughly and keep students focused on the intended learning. Some students, especially those with learning disabilities, can complete a whole exercise correctly but miss the point entirely. To overcome this you must direct their attention to the learning focus and ask them to explain it. You should not accept a non-specific response. Here is an example of a student explaining the learning focus through reflective dialogue:

Teacher: What were you learning here, Jack?

Jack: 'E' on the end of words.

Teacher: Yes. And what's the rule about them?

Jack: (Long silence) The 'e' makes the other vowel say its name.

Teacher: That's absolutely right. Can you show me one and how it works?

Jack: This one, 'game'. The 'e' makes the 'a' say 'a'. Otherwise it would be 'gam'.

Teacher: I couldn't explain better myself.

Jack: Thanks.

Supporting writing tasks

To help avoid errors, you can provide reference word lists, such as:

- 135 Most used words (see Appendix 4)
- 330 Frequently used words (see Appendix 5).

You can also create your own lists to meet the needs of your students.

To help students spell an unknown word correctly, teach different ways to spell a sound. Students can also refer to the Different ways to spell a sound (see Appendix 6). This shows the range of letter patterns used for particular sounds and limits choices of spelling possibilities. Students invariably choose the correct one.

Using a computer word processor can be very beneficial for building confidence and motivation, increasing speed legibility for some students, and reducing (but not eliminating) spelling errors through use of a spell checker. Some software programs that provide word banks are also popular and useful for students with severe learning difficulties.

Thorough, enthusiastic, interesting and challenging teaching is the key to improving your students' spelling. This book will help you select appropriate ways to implement action.

Chapter 1

Errors, causes and action to take

In this chapter error types are discussed and action suggested. A quick error analysis spreadsheet is provided in Appendix 1.

Error type: high frequency words

High frequency words are those written most often by most people. It is important that children learn these words correctly before errors become learnt and hard to undo. When you embark on a spelling recovery programme, errors in high frequency words need to be anticipated and addressed as soon as they are noticed.

Action

- Ensure that students who cannot spell all of the high frequency words (appropriate for their age) have a reference list handy while writing (see Appendix 4 and Appendix 5).
- Draw attention to these words in reading texts. (For example, you could play a game against the clock of 'Find the word'.)
- Work through the words systematically so that students memorise all of them. Some students will need to go over them many times before they are thoroughly learnt.
- Use an effective memorising strategy. 'Look, cover and write' can be used, although many students do not use it effectively. You could choose a more multi-sensory method. The CHIMP strategy (see Appendix 2) meets the needs of most learners for better retention.

Error type: irregular or difficult spelling

There are some typical words that are often misspelt because of irregular or difficult spelling. Irregular words include 'friend'; 'eye'; 'school'; and 'yacht'. Particularly difficult words include (depending on age) the 'ough' words; double letters (such as 'hoping'/'hopping'); 'done' and homophones (such as 'pear'/'pair').

Possible causes

There is a range of possible causes when students have problems spelling irregular or difficult words:

- Students may be unaware of the irregularity or difficulty.
- Students may not commit the spelling to memory.
- Students do not use mnemonic strategies.
- Students may have given up trying.

Action

You can adopt different strategies to attempt to deal with the problem of irregular or difficult spelling. The strategy chosen should reflect the extent of the problem, as well as a student's personal learning needs.

- Make time to teach and provide practice for the irregular and difficult high frequency words.
- Draw attention to (or ask students to find) the irregular spelling in the words.
- Help students to memorise the words through an effective strategy.
- Help students to practise the spelling with games as well as written exercises. (No student is too old to play a game and a few minutes in an activity with an element of fun or competitiveness may reinforce the spelling.)

Error type: phonetic spelling

Simple phonetic spelling indicates an early developmental stage in spelling learning and indicates real problems in older students.

Simple phonetic spelling is logical – the writer reproduces the sound of the word on a letter-by-letter basis. One letter is written for each separate spoken sound, for example writing 'alafnt' for 'elephant'. This sort of spelling reflects a student's knowledge of the relationship between sounds and letters and is vital for the development of good spelling. Five-year-old students who spell this way show progress, but older students who spell this way demonstrate arrested learning about spelling.

A typical example of incorrect phonetic spelling is sound–perfect single letter representation. Common mistakes include:
- 'plat' for 'plate' (logical when using the name sound of 'a')
- tn' for 'ten' (logical when using the name of 'n' for the sound 'en')
- 'wos' for 'was'
- 'difrent' for 'different'
- 'unessery' for 'unnecessary'.

Another example of simple phonetic spelling is 'not quite right' sound representation. This kind of mistake includes:
- 'dut' for 'dart'
- 'pat' for 'bat'
- 'defnet' for 'definite'.

Possible causes

- Students may not understand that words are not always spelt with single letters representing sounds.
- Students may not even write the sounds phonically. These students may have more complex difficulties, probably in auditory processing, that is in listening to the separate sounds and writing them correctly.
- Students may not understand or have correctly learnt which letter patterns represent some sounds (the 'not quite right' representation shown above).
- Students may not understand morphemes (the structure of words such as prefix, base word and suffix) and thus not know how to structure the word.
- Students may not understand etymology (the development of the word) and thus not know how the different parts of the word should connect together.

Other causes may be because:
- Students have not have been taught the components of spelling beyond the names of letters.
- Errors in the early stages of writing may not have been rectified and these errors have become learned through habit.

Action

Concepts and strategies

- Explain that every chunk (syllable) in English needs a vowel (or vowel letter pattern if vowels are omitted). Teach students to check their words for too many consonants in a row.
- Teach students high frequency, difficult words thoroughly. You cannot assume that students will learn the spelling of any words by completing exercises using the words. Although contextual use is vital, students do not necessarily learn the spelling from this because their concentration is on the context. For many students, the spelling (especially of difficult words) must be discussed and memorised, then practised and tested, with a focus on the spelling. You might consider providing practice exercises and fast games to consolidate learning. Special activities to help students remember the letter patterns of the difficult or irregular parts within words may also be helpful.
- Teach students how to tackle the spelling of an unknown word they are going to use. (See Appendix 3.)
- Once students have grasped the basics, consider introducing them to the meaning families (etymology); prefix, suffix and base word concepts (morphemes) and how to apply this knowledge. (See Morphemes and etymology section on page 9.)
- Provide appropriate reference lists of high frequency words so that students reduce their learnt errors in writing tasks. These lists should be displayed prominently so students are comfortable referring to them (see Appendix 4 and Appendix 5).

Incorrect sound-letter association

Students need to learn the range of representations of sounds by single letters and by letter patterns such as 'ee', 'th', 'ous':

*   Teach students the different spelling patterns for vowel sounds. For example, each single vowel either 'says':
    *   – its short sound: for example, 'a' for 'apple
    *   – its name sound: for example, 'a' in 'cake'
    *   – the sound of another vowel (this occurs in relatively few words): for example, 'a' in 'was' or 'o' in 'come'.
*   You may need to provide direction in listening to ensure that students can identify the differences between the single vowel sounds, which are often confused. For example, some students cannot hear, without training, the difference between the sounds of 'cat' and 'cut'; 'pat' and 'pet'; 'peg' and 'pig', 'seek' and 'sick'.
*   Ensure students learn the regular sounds in both groups of vowels thoroughly. The term 'name vowel sound' is more practical than 'long vowel sound' because 'name sound' can be applied as a sorting device, particularly. This is especially important when adding a suffix. Play games and explore texts for examples.
*   Teach 'y' as a vowel as well as a consonant. As a short vowel sound, 'y' says 'i' as in 'cylinder'. As a name sound, it says 'i' as in 'sky' and 'e' as in 'happy'.

For students who use simple phonetic spelling, also refer to Wrong order, omissions, additions, substitutions and limited phonetic approximations (see page 10).

Error type: incorrect choice of letter pattern or homophone

Word errors in this category are usually spelt with more sophistication than simple phonetic errors. Students select a possible but wrong letter pattern or whole word. Refer to spelling rules (see Appendix 8) for teaching handy rules, such as the 'i before e' rule.

Typical examples of the wrong choice of a pattern include:
*   'mowse' for 'mouse'
*   'theif' for 'thief'
*   'rouph' for 'rough'.

Typical examples of the wrong choice of homophones include:
*   'see' for 'sea'
*   'there' for 'they're' or 'their'.

These also include 'look–alike' words such as 'were' for 'where'.

Action

Letter patterns

*   Introduce, as fast as possible, the fifty or so letter patterns such as 'ar', 'ch', 'tion'. Students also improve in reading skills – an additional advantage of your efforts. You

can refer students to Different ways to spell a sound (see Appendix 6) for writing unknown words. The chart provides most of the alternative ways to spell particular sounds within sample words. An example is the name sound of 'e', for which alternatives are 'tree', 'me', 'sea', 'key', 'thief', 'receive'. Students often choose the correct letter pattern when they see it.

- Teach students letter patterns by grouping words together: for example, 'ou' is used in the words 'house', 'loud' and 'round'. Commercial spelling programmes are excellent resources for these word groups.
- Encourage students to link the words back into context, and reinforce memory with a writing activity where the student puts all the words into one silly story: for example, 'The louse pounded loudly on the door of the round house. A mouse found him, pounced on him and ground him into flour.'
- Facilitate reinforcement of learning through word games and word building with letter cards.

Homophones and other words that 'look alike'

- Teach homophones and 'look-alike' words together as a contrasting pair (or group) when an error is noticed. Be careful to draw students' attention to both the similarities and differences in the words. It may be a good idea to introduce appropriate pairs and groups gradually throughout the year. It is particularly important for students to understand what the words mean and to think of how they will remember the differences in spelling and applied use. For example: the homophone group: 'there', 'their' and 'they're'.
- Encourage students to apply memory tricks such as: 'There' has 'here' in it. 'Their' always has a 'something' word after it (for example 'their dog'). 'They're' means 'they are'. For example: a student wants to write 'We are going there'. To decide which word is the correct one to use, the student can ask the following questions.
  1 Am I saying 'they are'? 'We are going they are.' No, that sounds wrong, so it's not 'they're'.
  2 Am I saying 'their + something'? 'We are going their … (something).' No, so it's not 'their'.
  3 Does it make sense to say 'here' instead? 'We are going here.' That sounds better, so it must be 'there'.

Error type: incorrect use of spelling rule or convention

Spelling 'rules' are generalities that, when learnt, help people to spell many words correctly without having to commit them separately to memory. Errors occur when students do not apply or incorrectly apply a particular 'rule' or convention of spelling.

Doubling consonants

This type of error usually involves doubling letters unnecessarily, or failing to double letters when it is required.

Typical examples of unnecessary doubling include:
- 'tapping' for 'taping'
- 'dissinterested' for 'disinterested'.

Typical examples of failing to double letters include:
- 'shoping' for 'shopping'
- 'unecessary' for 'unnecessary'.

Possible causes

Many of the words that are commonly subject to this type of error have prefixes or suffixes. Students may not properly understand the concept of adding a suffix or prefix to the base word. In some cases, the problem may be related to the vowel sound.

Action

Ensure students understand the concept of a base word, prefix and suffix. Teach students how to attach prefixes and suffixes correctly to base words, as follows.

Adding a prefix

To add a prefix (such as 're', 'in' or 'un') to a base word, all you do is write the prefix and then the word.

For example:
- re + submit = resubmit
- un + believable = unbelievable
- dis + appointment = disappointment.

Sometimes this means that two of the same letters are placed side by side: for example 'dis+satisfied', 'mis+spent', 'un+necessary'. When these double letters are vowels, then they can be separated with a hyphen, although nowadays, this rule is not always applied.

For example:
- co+operation = co-operation or cooperation

Adding a suffix

When adding a suffix that starts with a consonant, for example 'less', 'ment', just add it to the end of the word if the suffix starts with a consonant.

For example:
- hope + less = hopeless
- hand + ful = handful
- base + ment = basement.

But if the base word ends with a 'y', then:

a change the 'y' to an 'i'

b add the suffix.

For example:
- happy + ness = happiness
- pretty + est = prettiest.

When adding a suffix that starts with a vowel, for example 'ed', 'ing', 'er', double the consonants before adding the suffix when the base word or last chunk has a short vowel sound. The two consonants 'make' the vowel keep its short sound.

For example:
- pat + ed = patted
- run + ers = runners
- big + er = bigger
- stop + ed = stopped
- begin + ing = beginning.

If the word already ends with two consonants, for example 'send', you just add the suffix = sending.

Note: If the base word ends in an unstressed vowel chunk with 't' or 'p' on the end, then do not double the consonant. For example:
- credit + ed = credited
- benefit + ing = benefiting
- profit + ing = profiting
- gossip + ed = gossiped.

When adding to a word such as 'tape', delete the 'e' from the end of the base word and add the suffix, if the suffix starts with a vowel and the base word or last chunk has a name vowel chunk. The single consonant 'makes' the vowel keep its name sound.

For example:
- type + ed = typed
- save + ed = saved
- hate + ing = hating
- hope + ing = hoping.

Note: When the word has a 'soft' 'g' or 'c', keep the 'e'.

For example:
- trace+ able = traceable
- manage + able = manageable
- service + able = serviceable.

When the base word has a letter pattern just add the suffix.

For example:
- read + ing = reading
- fish + ed = fished
- cool + er = cooler.

See also Error type: Morphemic or etymological errors (page 9).

Error type: incorrect use of apostrophes

Judging by the spread of 'aprostrophitis' (a rash or complete absence of the little squiggles), apostrophes seem to be a big problem – although they need not be. The causes are lack of understanding, focus and strategies.

Action

Explain that the apostrophe has two uses.

1 It can be used to show ownership.

For example:

– the boat belonging to Michael = Michael's boat

– the meeting of all the parents = the parents' meeting.

Make sure students know that if the noun ends in the letter 's', the word may indicate only that the noun is plural and therefore does not need an apostrophe.

Teach students that there are three simple steps involved in using apostrophes for ownership correctly:

	Singular	Plural
a Write the owner (or owners)	the boy	the three boys
b Add an apostrophe at the end of the owner(s)	the boy'	the three boys'
c Add an extra 's' after the apostrophe if you think it sounds right	the boy's	the three boys'★
d Write the item that is owned	the boy's boat	the three boys' boat

★Note: There is no 's' added after 'the three boys' because it would not sound right. You can call the missing 's' the phantom 's'.

2 The contraction apostrophe shows where letters are omitted.

For example:
- 'do not' can be written as 'don't'
- 'they are' can be written as 'they're'
- 'I am' can be written as 'I'm'
- 'can not' can be written as 'can't'.

The apostrophe shows where the omitted letter (or letters) should be. Remind students that the apostrophe does not show where the words join up but indicates that there are missing letters.

Error type: morphemic or etymological errors

Morphemes are the structural elements of a word, and the connections made between the different parts of each word. Etymology is concerned with the meanings and historical origins of words. Morphemic or etymological errors are those that reflect a lack of understanding of the basis of a word. Students display better spelling skills when they are aware of both morphemes and etymology, as they often overlap.

Typical errors include:
- 'unecessary' for 'unnecessary'
- 'disatisfaction' for 'dissatisfaction'
- 'hopet' for 'hoped'
- 'bycicle' for 'bicycle'
- 'defenite' for 'definite'.

Action

Encourage students to explore the morphemic structure of words (such as base word, prefix and suffix). When students understand structure, they can spell multisyllabic words quite easily.

For example:
- 'unnecessary' = un + necessary
- 'dissatisfied' = dis + satisfied
- 'uninterested' = un + interested.

See also rules about prefixes and suffixes on page 6.

Teach students the etymology or definitions of word families. If students understand these, they can reap dividends in spelling accuracy.

For example, spelling the word 'bicycle' is easier when students understand that it is a blend of the word 'bi' meaning 'two' and 'cycle'. The word 'definite' is easier to spell correctly when students think of the base word 'define', and then add the ending.

Examples of word families that aid spelling because the trickiest letter is obvious in one word of the group include:
- author–authorise–authority–authorisation
- demonstrate–demonstration–demonstrative
- differ–difference–different
- critic–criticism–criticise

Explain the origin of strangely spelt words to students. This can be useful for students when remembering unfamiliar letter combinations, or that the word is not spelt as it sounds.

For example:
- 'spaghetti' comes from Italian ('spaga', string)
- 'yacht' comes from Dutch ('jaghtschip', pirate ship).

Error type: incorrect order, omission and addition of letters, limited phonetic approximations

Even good spellers occasionally make errors of order, omission and addition of letters, through a lapse of concentration or writing (or typing) too fast. Students who have the most serious spelling difficulties often mangle words terribly – invert letter order, add wrong letters, omit letters or use very limited phonetic spelling.

Typical errors using letters in the wrong order include:
- 'form' instead of 'from' and vice versa
- 'was' instead of 'saw' and vice versa
- 'siled' instead of 'slide'
- 'firend' instead of 'friend'.

Typical errors of letter omission, addition, and/or substitution include:
- 'Austria' instead of 'Australia'
- 'fight' instead of 'fright'
- 'excrshn' instead of 'excursion'
- 'whitch' instead of 'which'.

Errors of limited phonetic approximation are often hard to translate, even in contextual writing. Typical examples of such errors include:
- 'sruch' instead of 'surface'
- 'berful' instead of 'beautiful'.

Possible causes

There are various reasons for this type of spelling problem, including those listed for simple phonetic spelling (see page 2) and some require similar action:

- Students may not understand the phonic base of the written system – that people write something for each sound in a word, in the order in which they say the word. This causes students to use letters in the wrong order, or attempt phonetic approximations.
- Students may understand typical word structure (such as the need for a vowel in every chunk) and will then omit, substitute or use additional letters, or rely on phonetic approximations.
- Students write from visual memory only without listening.
- Students find it difficult to concentrate on the spelling of words due to distractions and concentration on the writing.
- Students have learned the errors too well through continually writing them.
- Students have poor speech articulation, or are unable to process the sounds.
- Students are confused over the visual similarity between some words and rely on partial memory of the word.

Action

Despite your teaching, some students will continue to make these types of errors when distracted, under pressure or concentrating very hard on content. However, many of these errors can be minimised by consistent and thorough teaching strategies.

Auditory strategies

Current research has identified the importance of well-developed phonological skills for the acquisition of reading and spelling. You may need to develop students' listening skills so they can process and write each bit of a word. This can be done in the context of regular learning, that is while you are studying particular words with them and when you notice relevant errors. There are a variety of different strategies that can be adopted.

- Encourage students to speak as clearly as possible. If necessary, you may need to exaggerate the formation of sounds or use a mirror.
- Encourage students to notice the physical changes in the mouth, tongue or throat as they say the sounds within a word. You should remind students that each change is represented in writing by a separate letter or group of letters. You can refer to Cued Articulation[6] for extra visual assistance, if needed, to support this learning.
- Emphasise chunking, that is the auditory break-up of syllables. For example, the word 'interesting' breaks up into 'in-ter-est-ing'.
- Remind students who have learning difficulties to say every word to themselves (aloud if possible) as they write it. They can learn to consciously make the voice tell the hand what to write (without letting their voices run on ahead). Discourage students from spelling out by letter names, except for any words that they have already learned correctly this way.

Visual strategies

Visual strategies are important for learning high frequency words. Encourage students to think of ways to make boring, functional words more interesting to learn. You can do this in a variety of ways:

- Students can colour or decorate the trickiest part of the word.
- Students can group high frequency words that have the same letter patterns.
- Students can make up sets of cards of the difficult words written in various ways. For example, for learning 'was' and 'saw':

| WAS | was | was | was | was | was |
| SAW | saw | saw | saw | saw | saw |

To sort such words as 'were' and 'where', cards display the word to be learned in context. For example:

We were
WERE HERE
Where are you?
Where has

They were
were at home
I know where
where was

You were
were going
Leave it where it is

- Students draw around the outside shape of the word and add appropriate graphic details to reinforce the meaning of the word.

For example:

Metacognitive strategies

Metacognition concerns awareness of one's own thinking and the planning and use of deliberate thinking tools. Metacognitive strategies underpin learning to learn and are important to teach, especially to students with learning difficulties who tend to be weak in this strategy area.

One example is the effective CHIMP strategy (see Appendix 2). As students work through this memorising thinking tool, they learn some of the other important concepts and strategies. A spelling 'rule' is another example of such a strategy.

Error type: miscellaneous errors

There are many other errors that do not fit precisely under the given categories:

1 Crossing words out. This indicates a form of editing that suggests the student has some idea of the spelling and needs more practice in the correct version.
2 Not attempting to spell some words. Students may give up trying because the effort is not worth the bother and they want to avoid lots of red slashes and having to rewrite. It is safer to write less, or not at all.
3 Writing oddly or very slowly. (See posture and poor handwriting page 17).
4 Not checking, even when this is suggested.

Students are often not taught how to proof-read. Even so, poor spellers find this difficult until they start learning about spelling in detail. Impress the importance of editing and teach students to edit for one thing at a time with spelling being the last item.

Action

There are many strategies that can be used to support the reluctant poor speller:

- Provide students with a reference list of words. This should include a list of frequently used words as well as key words and subject words.

- Encourage students to draw up a mind chart (also known as a mind map or concept map) when preparing to write on a topic. The mind chart should obviously include key words for which spelling guidance can be given. The mind chart helps to extend the students' ideas as well as providing students with the correct spelling for the writing task.
- Teach students strategies to help them write unknown words (see Strategies on page 47). Students who use effective strategies will produce spelling that is more likely to be correct.
- Teach students how to use a dictionary. Those with no idea of spelling will not find a dictionary particularly useful as a spelling tool but they do need to know how to use one. If students have some idea of how to spell a word, but are unsure if they are correct, a dictionary may be useful.
- Teach students the system of working through a word alphabetically. Some students will need to have a copy of the alphabet handy while doing this, and a few will still require an alphabet even when older.
- Make sure students understand how to use the short-cut reference words at the top of the dictionary pages.
- Make sure students know that some words will be listed under their base word. For example, to find the word 'particularly', it is necessary to look under 'particular'.
- Assess whether changes should be made to the learning environment. Students may be more successful when seated near the front of the room, facing the board.

Note: If you suspect visual or auditory problems, you should contact parents and suggest professional assessment.

Aside from the specific errors discussed above, there are other factors that can cause a variety of spelling problems. These require separate discussion and different strategies.

Chapter 2

Additional factors to consider

English is the student's second language

A non-English-speaking background (NESB) can be a major factor in spelling difficulties.

Possible causes

There are two types of languages: phonic (letters representing sounds) and iconic (words represented by stylised pictures). For students familiar only with the iconic, English spelling is very challenging. Even if the language spoken in the student's home is phonic based, English can still be difficult because of all the exceptions. Students with strong accents cannot always hear an accurate representation of how a word should sound.

Students who were born in another country may have had their schooling interrupted for a variety of reasons.

Action

- Try to learn something about the language of origin of these students. Are there particular sounds or letter groups that are likely to be difficult? For example, the sounds 'r' and 'l' pose particular problems for many students from Asian countries.
- Teach students the basics of spelling as quickly as possible.

The student has an identified disability

There are students integrated into regular classrooms who may be affected by physical, intellectual, emotional or behavioural disabilities and those with identified specific learning disabilities. Obviously, such students will need extra help but they are capable of learning.

Action

Find out students' strengths and learning preferences. For instance, is a particular student better at learning through visual, auditory, tactile or movement modalities? Be sure to include strategies that suit the student's strengths and refer to goals set out in the student's programme.

Auditory and visual difficulties

Students with problems with the auditory and visual aspects of the task will usually have spelling difficulties. Vision, hearing, visual and auditory processing and memory are all involved in spelling.

Possible causes

If you know impairment in hearing or vision is the problem, you can cater for the student. Watch out for students who may have unidentified problems. Energy is wasted by the learner in coping with, for instance, long-sightedness or differences in the focus of each eye or uneven eye tracking that may affect a student's ordering of the letters. Imperfect vision on its own is unlikely to be responsible for spelling difficulties but inadequate hearing is more significant.

Action

- Look out for signs of problems. For instance, check vision when students bend too closely, squint or frown, hold the book out a long way when reading, write with their head tilted, or lean sideways.
- Hearing may need checking when students do not follow instructions or ask you to repeat what you have said, speak very softly or very loudly, or mumble. Sometimes students seem unable to identify all sounds, such as the differences between vowels and in blending, for example 'bl', 'sc', 'fr'.
- Make environmental adaptations to suit students. Remember to place students with visual or auditory limitations where they can see and hear easily — usually to the side that favours their 'good' ear or eye. Enlarge text and notes on the board for students with limited sight. Keep the classroom as quiet as possible for students with limited hearing. For severely disabled students, Cued Articulation[7] is helpful in providing a hand gesture for each sound.
- Speech can sometimes be improved when students hear themselves reading or talking on tape.
- In your teaching, use multisensory approaches whenever possible and train students to use all their senses. That is, present information that the student sees and hears and says and does or manipulates. In practice, this might mean the student writes a group of words in colours, practises visualising (as in the CHIMP strategy), listens to and says the separate sounds, makes words with letter cards or plays a game to practise.

Poor cognitive processing, auditory, visual and working memory

Although they can see and hear well enough, students with spelling difficulties invariably have poor cognitive processing. Sometimes the student is just very slow to process thinking.

If ten to thirty seconds is needed for a student to think through a question (verbal or written) and then a response, the student experiences only confusion if interrupted by the question being repeated or put differently. Invariably, teachers don't interact much with these students because it 'takes too long' or teachers think they do not have any worthwhile contribution. Such students tend to write and copy slowly, too, despite possibly being very intelligent in other ways.

Possible causes

Some students have very limited short-term auditory memory (STAM) and/or visual memory (STVM). Since both are necessary in spelling, it is important to help such students as much as possible to avoid overload and provide encouragement.

Students with learning difficulties often have a poor working memory. Working memory allows for simultaneous performance of skills. When students are writing, attention must be shared between thinking of content matter, how to order and say it, spelling, punctuation and, for some, posture and handwriting. When any of these aspects of the task is a challenge, especially if the working memory is inefficient, something has to give!

Action

- Support students by setting up the environment to minimise confusion. Providing the same environment as you provide for those with impaired visual and hearing impairment often helps.
- Teach students to break up words into visual and auditory chunks. This is one of the most helpful strategies, and aids reading too.
- Limit the amount of detail in instructions. With oral instruction, suggest that students visualise themselves doing the task as you describe it.
- When dictating notes or helping students prepare for an essay, guide correct spelling with direct or indirect information. For instance, you might spell out very difficult words directly but help with others by sounding out in chunks ('en-vi-ron-ment') or by saying the spelling sounds ('fri-end).
- Use dictation as a tool for memory training. Dictation is also useful for teaching punctuation. Train students to mentally rehearse and, if they forget a bit, to leave a space and wait for the final reread to fill it (rather than getting completely lost and left behind).[8]
- Encourage students to develop mnemonics (memory 'tricks') and deliberately include emotions to help remember. For example, most people remembered 'yacht' by saying the word as 'yach et'. Children remember 'friend' by saying 'I fri the end of my friend'. This includes emotion, too, which strengthens the recall.

Refer also to ideas in Error type: Phonetic spelling (see page 2) and Error type: Incorrect order, omissions and addition of letters, limited phonetic approximations (see page 10).

Undeveloped strategic thinking skills

Metacognition, the awareness of one's own thinking process and deliberate use of strategic thinking, is essential for the rapid development of spelling skills but is often lacking in some students.

Possible causes

Students with learning difficulties tend to be unaware of their own thinking processes. These students do not realise that strategies can be used to help them reason through different tasks and assume that other people just 'know the answers' through some magic or superior intelligence.

Teachers do not always teach metacognitive strategies of 'how to learn' and 'what to say to yourself'.

Action

- Encourage students to talk themselves through their thinking processes to help them understand and remember. Students can make posters about these strategies to remind themselves and you need to keep reminding them, too.
- Teach visual and verbal mnemonics, which are mental tricks to aid memory. For example, a visual mnemonic is remembering the word 'eye' by drawing in two eyes and a nose on the word. One verbal memory trick is a rhyming rule, such as 'i' before 'e' and swap after 'c', when the sound is 'ee'.
- Encourage students to make up their own strategies and to share these strategies with others. Ask students to articulate what they are learning or have learned from particular exercises. This makes them focus on the learning and gives you valuable information on the level of their understanding.
- Teach students spelling terminology (such as letter names, short and name vowel sounds, prefix, suffix, base word, etc.), and the tools to explain and discuss spelling. For example, when a student has spelt 'shopping' as 'shoping', instead of just telling the student there should be two 'p's', you can use this as a teaching moment. 'Is the vowel in "shop" a short or name sound? So, what's the rule when you add a suffix/ending? That's right, it needs two consonants before the ending.'
- Teach students the CHIMP strategy (see Appendix 2) and Strategy to write an unknown word (see Appendix 3) and to refer to relevant word lists and a dictionary appropriate to their level. Teach them the rules of spelling (see also Spelling rules and ways to remember, Appendix 8).

Poor handwriting

Since the daily teaching of handwriting has disappeared from many classrooms and children are encouraged to write freely, many students do not form letters properly (that is efficiently).

They start letters, such as 'a', 'o' and 'd' in the 'wrong' place and go around in the 'wrong' direction, which makes joining awkward. They may also start letters such as 'n' and 'r' at the bottom instead of the top, which is slow.

Possible causes

- Poor handwriting can have a number of causes such as poor fine motor control, left-handedness, lack of wrist flexibility and/or coordination. Students may have a tight, inefficient grip of the pen. The writing paper may be on too much of a slant, or not enough.
- Some students find cursive (joined) writing much harder to write than printed letters.
- Bad posture can exacerbate poor writing. Scoliosis or kyphosis (curvatures of the spine) can cause the posture or it may indicate vision problems. (For example, leaning sideways may enable students who are short-sighted in one eye and long-sighted in the other to see more clearly what they are writing.)

Action

- Encourage students to participate in activities that improve coordination and muscle control. These might include sport, playing a musical instrument, gymnastics, karate or brain gym exercises.
- Teach handwriting skills, even to older students, who will usually make some changes, especially when they appreciate the benefit of forming letters efficiently.
- Encourage the use of a keyboard, especially for students with slow or illegible handwriting.
- Encourage 'correct' pen grip (which does not include thumb wrap-around). Encourage students to hold the pen in a way that enhances the flow of writing, that is with the pen resting in the hollow between thumb and forefinger. Stranglehold grip may lead to arthritis – another reason to present to the student. However, it is usually counter-productive to try to change a student who is very comfortable with an odd style of handwriting and who writes fast and neatly.
- Remember that most students write better on lines (and between lines when learning).
- Help students who write very untidily with erratic vertical slopes. Ask them to place a ruler or pen on each vertical slope to observe the slopes. Then explain that, in neat writing, vertical strokes are all parallel. Students often improve rapidly when a sheet of vertical donkey lines (slanted at the best angle for the individual) is placed under their writing pages for a few days.
- Remind students to sit with good posture. Their backs should be straight, with feet flat on the floor, and they should be sitting back into their chairs. The improvement in their handwriting when they sit up straight is often remarkable.
- Help struggling left-hand students to develop the best arm position possible. The arm should be held at the side of the writing or just below it, rather than above.
- Check that the paper is placed on the table correctly. Right-handers are usually more comfortable with the paper angled to the right; and left-handers are more comfortable with the paper angled to the left. A raised sloping surface also helps.

- Place displays of correctly written letters around the room so that students can copy them.

Slant for left-handers   Slant for right-handers

- Suggest that students change the type of pen they use. Some students write better using a felt-tipped pen or one of the more expensive alternatives to the cheap biro. A padded finger rest often helps, too.

Environmental and teaching factors

Blaming the student is very easy when looking for reasons for failure and, sometimes, there are contributing factors within the student. But poor physical and emotional environments and teaching approaches often create or exacerbate students' lack of attention and lack of knowledge.

Possible causes

- The environment of the classroom is often distracting. Some students, particularly those with Attention Deficit Disorder, will attend to everything (except what you want them to do). Distractions include noises inside and outside the classroom, such as talking, traffic and movement of any sort.
- Students may think (or know) because of past experiences, that they cannot do the work and so do not even try. While most teachers are encouraging, some are not. Students are told to 'tell me when you don't understand', yet some teachers, even in these days of an informed society, sometimes refuse to help saying, 'You should know that.'
- The work may not be interesting enough to engage students.
- Teachers are not always clear in their own mind about the desired focus or do not explain it to students adequately. It is easy to forget that something is only easy for you because you already know it and have absorbed it thoroughly into your knowledge base.
- Students with learning difficulties often miss the point of the learning even while 'getting it right'. Their focus is often 'on the trees' rather than 'on the woods'.

Action

- Decide on the key focus of the learning and explain this to students. For example, 'Today you are going to write about a personal experience. The main focus is on planning out three paragraphs before writing.' Limit the focus for students with learning difficulties, especially for first drafts. For any task that has challenging content, focus initially on content rather than spelling. In the short term, until students spell well automatically, provide a reference base for relevant correctly spelt words – either a list or the words written on a mind chart of content.

- Make the learning as relevant as possible. Explain the value of the task to students.
- Involve students in setting up the task. For example, ask students to suggest some of the words to be included and ask them to write these on the board.
- Make the task as interesting as possible. If the task is challenging and fun, it is more likely to be effectively learnt. Introduce an element of 'game' into practice learning.

Chapter 3

Questions asked about students with severe learning difficulties

Some students demonstrate severe learning difficulties in spelling, which can stem from inherent (possibly inherited) learning difficulties. Often, teachers lack resources and time and may feel they are making little progress, even when they do help. However, analysing the number and type of errors made and following this up systematically will generally show that you have made a difference.

The problems are partly due to teaching that was neither specific nor explicit enough.

Some common questions

The difficulty with constructing a list of questions like this is that the answers often depend on circumstances. Thus there are no absolutely 'right' answers. However, the following suggestions can act as a guide.

Where do I start?

Start first by assessing and analysing students' spelling. You should make an effort to categorise both strengths and weaknesses. This will show you what area(s) of understanding and strategies need to be addressed.

Then, plan a programme that is not too complicated to be implemented and that can be easily reviewed and evaluated. It should aim, as far as possible, to help the student manage the class programme. You might utilise a commercial spelling programme, with thorough supervision and discussion on the learning focus of each exercise as a supplement.

Use the suggestions in previous chapters to help you devise strategies for particular problems. Teach students a strategy to memorise words and start teaching frequently used words immediately. If a student is failing spelling tests, the test word list makes another good starting point. As test performance improves, the student will increase in self-esteem and enthusiasm.

When working with older students, ask them to select the words they need. For a starter, ask students to write about something of interest or with which they are familiar and then find and underline any words that 'need fixing'. You could also add your own underlining. Students select words from the errors to memorise correctly.

Note: You should pay special attention to teaching students high frequency words.

What teaching methods are best?

No single teaching method is guaranteed to suit all students. However, the general principles that are most likely to work are outlined in the introduction of this book (see page viii) and briefly summarised here.

Focus on the goal

- Know exactly what you want students to learn from each activity and share this learning goal with them. If you are unsure about where you are heading, it will be confusing for students.
- If possible, assess and analyse each student's spelling and tailor a programme to suit their individual needs.

Use direct teaching

- Show students what to do and how to do it.
- Ask students what they already know and build on that knowledge. Ask students to explain things back to you. This shows students that you respect their knowledge and informs you of what you need to teach.
- Always be clear and explicit when giving instructions.
- Encourage students to think and concentrate. You could do this by challenging them, or by coming at the problem in a different way.
- Be creative in making a repetitive task more interesting. Games encourage faster learning because everyone likes fun and an element of competition. Snap and Noughts and Crosses, for instance, are very useful to practise learning that would otherwise be rather boring.
- Flashcards are useful for assessment and games. Plain playing cards can be purchased and are suitable for students of all ages. Use different colours to write on them as this can help students to associate different sound groups or letter chunks if they are in the same colour. These cards can be used for any number of spelling areas, including sound and letter patterns, defining homophones and adding suffixes.

Focus on metacognitive strategies

The spelling strategy is just as important as the content of the exercises. Strategies are especially important for students with learning difficulties.

- Students need to say a word as they write it rather than spelling it out by letter names. This synchronising of voice and hand helps produce letters in the correct order.
- Teach all the strategies described in this book, such as those to memorise and to spell an unknown word.
- At the end of a session, ask students what new knowledge they have gained. Do not accept a vague response. It is important to tease out the details as this helps develop metacognitive skills and establish the learning in a student's long-term memory.

Should I go more slowly?

If a student is a long way behind, you need to teach the basics as fast as possible and try to help the student with class work. In spelling, the same rules and strategies keep coming up over and over again, so you can teach them in the context of the student's other work at class level. You will probably need to supplement your 'in-context' teaching with exercises that focus on practice of the particular rule. This should be thoroughly planned – not just vague busy work – and might require additional staffing or home assistance.

Here is an example of the 'go as fast as you can' approach, with a new client of the author, a Year 11 student who has severe difficulties in literacy but is advanced in maths. As part of the second lesson, we developed a mind chart for a speech he is giving in English. This also provided data for detailed error analysis. Among the errors were two words that indicated he had no idea about how to add a suffix ('ed', 'ing'). Because this is important, we discussed the strategy immediately, he wrote a few relevant examples and took home some practice exercises, which will be followed up next time and the strategy revisited through his other work.

Keep the lesson moving. Students get restless if you are too slow or you talk for more than a minute without engaging them in response. At the same time, students with severe learning difficulties become very anxious if they feel you are rushing them! It is a fine balance. You should always give time – sometimes up to 30 seconds – for a student to answer a question. Train students to ask for further explanation, rather than interrupting their train of thought.

How much editing should I expect from students?

Students will put effort into editing if you stress its importance, show them how to do it correctly and acknowledge their efforts. Teach students to proof-read for spelling by asking them to underline any words they think may need fixing, then help students fix them.

Students should take advantage of a computer spell-check as a proof-reading tool, with the knowledge that all errors will not be picked up. However, very poor spellers are often frustrated because the spell-check cannot interpret their spelling and they hate 'all those horrible red lines'.

How much correction should I write on students' work?

It is important to be generous with ticks and positive comments. You should look at the content of the work before the spelling. If a student has made many spelling errors, underline all the errors (but not in red) and print at least the most important words correctly at the end of the piece of work. If you want students to benefit from your corrections, expect students to write out the words a few times and memorise them. Follow up.

Should I give spelling tests to students who have difficulties?

While there is a limit to the value of weekly spelling tests because the 'learning' may not always be applied subsequently in students' writing, tests do provide students with a high motivation to memorise the words and become more familiar with them. Generally, encourage students to learn the same words, or at least some of them, as the rest of the class. If you teach students how to memorise spelling, and make it worthwhile for them to apply the skill, they should be successful.

What about students who are very anxious?

Some students can be paralysed by a fear of being wrong. Students can also be affected by matters outside the classroom. It is important that you try to reduce students' anxiety levels. There are a variety of ways to do this:

• Try to sound relaxed and enthusiastic yourself.
• Acknowledge effort and point out any improvement.
• Acknowledge attempts to self-correct.
• Help students to give the 'right' answer. For example, you might start to say the first sound of the word and let them finish it off.
• When correcting errors, find a 'yes' in every correction. For example, when spelling words which have silent letter chunks you might say to a student, 'Yes, the way you have spelt it does make sense, This word is actually spelt with ...'. You could also acknowledge that the student's mistake is a common difficulty. For example, you might tell the student that 'Most people get that muddled'.
• Explain to students that any test is 'just to see what you know and what I need to teach you'.
• Some things just have to be learned by practice. Playing a game can be an effective way of doing this.
• Be ready to take the pressure off. For example, when students show signs of unproductive agitation by shaking their head, looking desperate, breathing unevenly or showing sudden restlessness, it may be a good idea to allow some time for relaxation. Trying to force learning at this stage will not achieve anything and may simply create setbacks.

Do students grow out of learning difficulties?

Students who are given appropriate encouragement and careful teaching can overcome their difficulties by developing other compensatory skills. Albert Einstein is a perfect example.

How do students with severe spelling difficulties cope in senior school?

Some students will put in extra effort at senior level to learn how to spell. Others can only cope with their set workload.

In some countries, students with severe literacy difficulties may be eligible for extra support, such as a scribe to write their answers in exams and/or for extra time. A full assessment by a psychologist is usually required. The use of a reader/scribe in Year 12 has made a significant difference to a student currently supported by the author. His self-esteem and confidence have increased considerably as well as his marks.

Chapter 4

Two case studies

The following two case studies show the sort of spelling recovery possible within an individualised, weekly programme. The studies recorded the progress of 'Margaret' and 'Stephen' over about 12 weeks of Term 1.

Margaret

At the time of initial testing Margaret was 10 years and 11 months of age and in Year 5. She had experienced learning difficulties throughout her schooling. She presented as shy but smiling, apparently well-adjusted, with a good sense of humour. She talked so fast that it was very hard to follow her speech. She was referred to the author by her previous specialist tutor (who had taken a position in Margaret's school).

Assessment

Margaret scored 30 (critical low score 31) on the South Australian Spelling Test with an equivalent average score of 8.1 years. When asked to 'think aloud' for four words, she sounded out 'chop' and 'ship' and spelt out 'food' and 'fire', all correctly.

Her responses to the diagnostic placement test 'Now I can spell and read better too' Curriculum Standards Framework Level 2 (B) (Roberts, 2000), indicated that she could start on Level 3 but needed some gaps filled from previous levels. It was significant that the only short vowel sound Margaret could correctly identify in isolation was 'o'. This was interesting, since her phonic spelling was fairly accurate in terms of vowel sounds.

The following passage is a typed version of Margaret's spelling in context assessment. The underlined words are those she identified when asked to select any words that 'might need fixing'. The 60-word passage contained eight errors (13 per cent of the total).

> *Were going on camp next week with the boy's. We are going to <u>Willsons pomtor</u> for a week, we will be sleeping in tents and going for a long bush ~~war~~ walk <u>tomorow</u> the boys are coming for a <u>barbq</u> at the school and the <u>senya</u> school pool will be open. but I not <u>dering</u> to swim with the boys.*

Error analysis

Margaret used her knowledge of phonics well but made errors with a number of fairly common words. Her knowledge of common letter patterns was hazy. She had a partially accurate knowledge of other words she would have encountered, for example 'wiman' and 'anser'.

'Spelling out' the letter names worked for words that may have been easily recalled, as did sounding out for others, perhaps those for which she knew the letter patterns ('ship' and 'chop'). More investigation is needed to increase her success rate.

Margaret's accuracy in selecting four of the eight errors in her own writing indicates that she has some visual knowledge of how words should look. Her phonetic spelling (for example 'Willsons pomtor') is a reasonably accurate reflection of her extremely rapid speech.

Planning Margaret's tutoring programme

Goal setting

Goal	Time frame
1 School weekly test Goal: To know how to spell the words in the weekly test at school	By the 3rd week
Goal: To memorise words using the CHIMP strategy (see Appendix 2)	By the 3rd week
2 Vowel sounds Goal: To know and identify the short and name vowel sounds	By the 3rd week
3 High frequency words Goal: To know the 300 most used words (in Roberts, 2000)	In 9 months
Goal: To memorise words using the CHIMP strategy (see Appendix 2)	In 9 months
4 Letter patterns Goal: To read all the letter patterns	In 3 months
Goal: To learn all the word groups in Level 3 (Roberts, 2000)	In 6 months
5 Rules and strategies Goal: To learn the strategies which are used when adding a vowel suffix	In 3 months
6 Rules and morphemic base Goal: To know and apply the concept of prefix, suffix and base word	In 9 months
7 Spelling in context Goal: To edit and find 90 per cent of errors	In 3 months
Goal: To reduce errors by 25 per cent	In 3 months
Goal: To remember how to spell words memorised previously	In 9 months

Spelling Error Analysis Record

Name ..*Margaret*.................................. Age ..*10 years 11 months*.......... Year ..*Level 5*............. Date ....

Misspelt words Student's spelling (+ correct spelling)	Word categories		Types of errors				More severe problems, if frequent errors here	
	High frequency word 135 or R = Relatively, for age	Irregular or difficult spelling I = Irregular D = Difficult, relative to age	Logical phonetic spelling	Incorrect choice *Vowel, Consonant, Letter pattern, Homophone*	Incorrect use of spelling rule or convention	Morphemic or etymological errors	Wrong order, Omission, Addition, Substitution, Limited approximation	Miscellaneous, e.g. *No attempt, Limited output, Crossing out, Copying problems*
dun (done)	✓ R		✓	✓ V o=u				
eney (any)	✓ R		✓	✓ V a=e				
grate (great)	✓ R			✓ Hom				
shore (sure)	✓ R			✓ Hom				
wiman (women)	✓ R	✓ I	✓	✓ Vs				
senya (senior)		✓ D	✓	✓ LP ior				
hoped	✓ R				✓ +ed			
wich (which)	✓ 135			✓ LP wh			✓ Om sil H	
fite (fight)				✓ LP igh				
were (We're)	✓ R	✓ D	✓		✓ Apos			
brekfst (breakfast)	✓ R		✓	✓ LP ea			✓ Om v	

Note relevant factors possibly contributing to errors

Major known:
e.g. English as second language, specific disability

Nil

Physical
e.g. Hearing, speech, vision, handwriting, posture

Nil

Intellectual, cognitive
e.g. Memory: auditory and visual, processing, attention, strategies, reading

M took a long time to think out each word. Reading a grade below age

Emotional
e.g. Anxiety, trauma, relationships

Nil

Environmental
e.g. Lighting, heat, cold, position in room, trauma, relationships

Nil

Note strengths shown and other beneficial factors

Student knowledge of content, strategies. Attitude

M knows single consonants and vowels (probably). M thinks before she writes.
Cheerful and willing to try.

Additional help available

Tutoring, extra help at school, class using CHIMP strategy to memorise too.

Other

Details of the programme

The time frame of the case study included the first 12 sessions of Margaret's programme. This was interrupted by the two-week first-term holiday. Several goals were addressed concurrently.

1 School weekly test
Goal: To know how to spell the words in the weekly test at school.
Goal: To memorise words using the CHIMP strategy (see Appendix 2).

Action and outcome

Margaret was introduced to the CHIMP strategy (see Appendix 2) in the second session, using the word 'tomorrow' from her camp text and 'breakfast' from her spelling list. She found the visualising step more difficult than most children do, but was eventually able to 'see' the words and spell them forwards and backwards. She then 'taught' her mother what she had learnt. This reinforced the practice at home, assessed her understanding and reinforced the learning.

Margaret continued to utilise this strategy very successfully to learn her spelling words for school tests. She also used the words she had learnt in her writing at school. Her test results rose from very low scores to high scores.

Evaluation

The goal was achieved.

2 Vowel sounds

Goal: To know and identify the short and name vowel sounds in isolation and when applied.

Action and outcome

Margaret constructed a chart of each set of the vowels (including 'y'), then chose her own words and illustrations for each vowel. This was begun in the second session and finished at home. Margaret displayed the chart on her wall so that she could 'learn' it. She knew the sounds and letters well by the next session, and gradually applied them more effectively in reading and writing single words.

Evaluation

The goal was achieved in isolation and was often applied.

3 High frequency words

Goal: To know the 300 most used words (in Roberts, 2000).
Goal: To memorise words using the CHIMP strategy (see Appendix 2).

Action and outcomes

Margaret started to work through the list of words by addressing five in each weekly session with the author, and learning more at home. However, for various reasons, this routine activity stalled.

Time was also spent with Margaret looking at the homophone group 'were', 'where' and 'we're', which arose from Margaret's story about the camp (see page 26). To learn the differences, Margaret wrote each word and discussed the different meanings and strategies to remember the spelling of each word. The author made a flap card to help explain to Margaret the use of the apostrophe in 'we're' (one side of the card had the full spelling of 'we are', with the 'a' cut out and the other side has an apostrophe on the flap). Margaret then went on to make cards for other words that use an omission apostrophe.

Evaluation

This goal was not fully achieved and, at the time of writing, needed to be addressed more consistently in an ongoing programme. The homophone group was understood and Margaret could apply the right one when reminded.

New goal

At this stage of the programme a new goal was introduced.

Goal: to know the purpose of a learning task.

This goal arose because Margaret was unable to say what she had been 'learning' when doing her spelling exercises for homework. She also had difficulty telling the author what she had learnt during each session.

Action and outcomes

Margaret's task was to ask herself in tutoring sessions, at home and at school, 'What am I supposed to be learning here?'. After the author introduced this idea to her, Margaret said that she used it at school and was able to tell what she was learning by looking at the title of a task page. Margaret also improved in her ability to identify and tell the author what she had learnt during the session.

Evaluation

This goal was achieved.

4 Letter patterns

Goal: To read all the letter patterns.
Goal: To learn all the word groups in Curriculum Standards Framework Level 3 of the 'Now I Can Spell' programme (Roberts, 2000).

Action and outcomes

There were about 50 letter patterns for Margaret to learn. To help Margaret learn to recognise letter patterns quickly, the author played Snap with her, using a full set of letter patterns and matching words (which included phonic as well as written letter pattern matches). Margaret experienced some difficulty remembering the letter pattern 'i o u s', so the author encouraged her to explore words with the letter patterns 'o u s' and 'i o u s'. Margaret then used these words in writing one silly story. She enjoyed doing this and used her imagination delightfully.

Margaret made very good progress, reading and spelling about 75 per cent of these words correctly after a few weeks. She also applied the learning to read an unknown word when reminded to recall the patterns.

Word groups for each of the letter patterns were introduced to Margaret in different sets of exercises. Margaret did one or two pages each week for homework, which the author corrected and discussed with her in each session.

Evaluation

This level of learning continued to progress at a moderate rate.

5 Rules and strategies

Goal: To learn the strategies which are used when adding a vowel suffix.

Action and outcomes

Margaret was shown the rules for adding suffixes and revised these each week. She was able to explain the strategy (that there should be two consonants after the short vowel sound in a word but only one consonant after a name vowel sound in a word) and read and explain the spelling correctly. The author used flap cards on which the base word is written separately from the suffix, with cuts to flap up or down the letters to be manipulated. Margaret wrote some of the words in silly sentences and practised reading and spelling words in games such as Noughts and Crosses and Battleships.

Margaret was given small amounts of homework, which was followed up thoroughly in the next session.

Evaluation

At the time of writing Margaret was stopping to think before writing these words when they were the focus of a sentence. General application should continue to improve with practice. Some students need to speed up – Margaret needs to slow down.

6 Rules and morphemic base

Goal: To know and apply the concept of prefix, suffix and base word.

Action and outcomes

To teach Margaret the conceptual structure of words, the author chose to use one word that arose in Margaret's writing. The author started with the base word 'belief', then made 'believe', 'believable', 'disbelief' and 'unbelievable'. Margaret was able to explain to the author how to add a prefix to a base word. She wrote the words into a story.

Evaluation

Margaret made a good start with understanding the concept. As words arise incidentally (and in the Investigate step of the CHIMP strategy, see Appendix 2), she will be able to continue to explore this idea.

7 Spelling in context

Goal: To edit and find 90 per cent of errors.
Goal: To reduce errors by 25 per cent.
Goal: To remember how to spell words memorised previously.

Action and outcomes

One approach to reducing errors was to ask Margaret to 'Think double' – to think about the spelling of each word as well as the content of her writing as a whole. She also needed to slow down her thoughts when writing. She used a chart that showed her different ways to spell a sound (see Appendix 6), which provided her with alternatives for spelling any particular sound (for example 'ee', 'ea', 'e-e'). Margaret usually chose the correct alternative.

The focus on one thing at a time when editing encouraged greater accuracy in detecting errors both with spelling and with punctuation. The text of 350 words (written at the end of three months of sessions) contained 24 errors, 7 per cent of the total.

Evaluation

It was interesting to compare the errors in Margaret's two written assessment texts. The 24 errors in the second text gave the appearance that little progress had been made. However when it was compared with the first text error percentage, it was clear that Margaret had progressed. Her rate of making errors had halved. This was very encouraging.

South Australian Spelling Test

At the end of 12 weeks of sessions, Margaret scored 34 on the South Australian Spelling Test (Westwood, 1999), which is approximately equivalent to other students 9.5 years of age, an increase of one year over this period of tutoring. Since the words correctly spelt on the test had not been addressed specifically, it can be assumed that Margaret was generalising her learning strategies successfully.

Comments on progress

Margaret missed two sessions due to illness and an excursion. She improved overall (one year's increase in 12 weeks) and the author continued to develop the established goals and extend her knowledge and use of letter patterns, high frequency words, editing and punctuation. Margaret's confidence also appeared to have increased.

Stephen

At the time of initial testing Stephen was 11 years and 10 months of age and in Year 6. His learning problems emerged in his first year of school. Stephen played the cornet in an orchestra and liked sport. In Year 1 he completed a Reading Recovery programme, his reading improved but his skills subsequently decreased. Stephen made little progress and in Years 4 and 5 he was tutored in reading by a speech therapist. She referred him to the author when he started Year 6. Stephen had no visual problems and his oral comprehension was good.

Stephen is left-handed. When he began working with the author his class teacher was giving him a special list of words to learn each week, with an exercise to practise using the words in context. This exercise comprised one set of words at about Year 2 Level in a particular letter pattern group, with an extra set of harder 'Champion' words containing the same letter pattern.

Assessment

Stephen scored 27 on the South Australian Spelling Test (SAST) (Westwood, 1999). The critical low score for Stephen's age is 35. His score was the equivalent of students who

Spelling Error Analysis Record

Name ..... *Stephen* .... Age ... *11 years, 10 months* ...... Year ... *Level 6* .... Date ....

Misspelt words Student's spelling (+ correct spelling)	Word categories		Types of errors				More severe problems, if frequent errors here	
	High frequency word 135 or R = Relatively, for age	Irregular or difficult spelling I = Irregular, D = Difficult, relative to age	Logical phonetic spelling	Incorrect choice *Vowel, Consonant, Letter pattern, Homophone*	Incorrect use of spelling rule or convention	Morphemic or etymological errors	Wrong order, Omission, Addition, Substitution, Limited approximation	Miscellaneous, e.g. *No attempt, Limited output, Crossing out, Copying problems*
h— (who)	✓ 135							✓
scim (seems)	✓ R			✓ *LP ee*			✓ *Add c* ✓ *Lim Ap*	
eney (any)	✓ R		✓	✓ *a=e*				
wiman (women)	✓ R	✓ *I*					✓ *Sub n for m* ✓ *Lim Ap*	
eie (eye)	✓ R	✓ *I*	✓	✓ *V*				
diging (digging)	✓ R		✓		✓ *Double g*			
cined (climbed)	✓ R			✓ *LP sil b*			*Om L* ✓ *Lim Ap*	
sarp (safe)	✓ R			✓ *LP a-e*			✓ *Lim App* ✓ *subst*	✓
donw (down)	✓ 135			✓ *LP ow*			✓ *wrong order*	
neant (nugget)				✓ *V, C*	✓ *Double g*		✓ *Lim App* ✓ *om Cs, syll*	
slart (splashed)	✓ R			✓		+ *ed*	✓ *Lim App, om* ✓ *Wr order*	
conpeutor (computer)	✓ R		✓ *almost*				✓ *sub m for n*	

Readers are permitted to photocopy this page. From *Spelling Recovery*, ACER Press © Copyright 2001, Janet Roberts.

Note relevant factors possibly contributing to errors

Major known:
e.g. English as second language, specific disability

Specific learning disability. Reading Recovery G1

Physical
e.g. Hearing, speech, vision, handwriting, posture

Handwriting extremely laboured. Left handed, over-the-top, moves hand every letter.

Speech: consonants blurred; does not always speak in full sentences.

Intellectual, cognitive
e.g. Memory: auditory and visual, processing, attention, strategies, reading

Errors suggest hearing or processing problem + DK letters that represent sounds.

Spells out, rather than sounding out.

Emotional
e.g. Anxiety, trauma, relationships

Understandably anxious. Has almost given up. Has been unwilling to do homework.

Environmental
e.g. Lighting, heat, cold, position in room, trauma, relationships

Nil

Note strengths shown and other beneficial factors

Student knowledge of content, strategies. Aattitude

S knows many of letters/sounds; has learned some HF words eg friends, fight.

Willing to try. IQ in average range, talks sensibly.

Additional help available

Tutoring

Other

Mother willing to help.

are 7.8 years of age, about four years behind the average level for his age. Stephen was asked to 'think aloud' as he wrote four of the words, to gauge whether he sounded out or spelt out. He spelt out (incorrectly) all of them.

Stephen's responses to the diagnostic placement test '*Now I can spell and read better, too*' Curriculum Standards Framework Level 2 (B) (Roberts, 2000), indicated that he should start on Level 1 of the programme. He needed to learn short vowel sounds, some consonant sounds, most letter patterns and how to read and spell blends. The following passage is the typed version of the spelling in context assessment, an 80-word text which was written by Stephen in a spidery script.

> *we went on an <u>exsient</u> to <u>soverhillit</u> toock 2 hours on a bas when we got theire we went <u>donw</u> a minen and it was could we lison to a <u>voce</u> and we cimed up and fid the <u>viese</u> we saw a big gold naent and a <u>conpeurtor</u> iniges of them diging it up and he slart water on it and it was big and we saw a rurak in a sarp and then we went up to the <u>srushs</u>.*

Translation: We went on an excursion to Sovereign Hill. It took two hours on a bus. When we got there, we went down a mine and it was cold. We listened to a voice and we climbed up and found the voice. We saw a big, gold nugget and computer images of them digging it up and he splashed water on it and it was big and we saw a replica in a safe and then we went up to the surface.

When asked to underline words he thought 'might need fixing', Stephen selected seven of the 18 errors. The total errors in this text were 22 per cent of the whole.

Other observations

In the time given to check his work, Stephen did not change any of his spelling.

Stephen was really struggling physically, to write with a jerky, 'over-the-top' left-handed style. He printed his writing, starting many of the letters from the 'wrong' starting point, at a speed approximating that of a 5-year-old. Stephen also moved his whole arm and shifted his grip with almost every letter. The level of effort required certainly would have reduced his ability to concentrate fully on either spelling or content.

In talking with Stephen, he often hesitated but always answered a question fully. His consonants were rather blurred when he was speaking, which may account partly for some of the missed sounds in his written spelling.

Based on a short, initial reading assessment, Stephen was assessed to be slow in oral reading but comprehension was appropriate for his age. (This was tested by asking Stephen to explain the passage. He provided all the details expected for the answers to the set questions.)

Error analysis

Stephen had broad-ranging spelling problems. Many of his words were unrecognisable. Some of his phonetic spelling reflected his blurry speech articulation, suggesting that he already had some idea of the link between sound and letter. Spelling out, rather than the more strategic method of sounding out unknown words, was ineffective for most words.

Stephen's lack of spelling skills was severe enough that he did not alter any of his attempts – either they looked all right to him or he did not know how else to write them. With his lack of knowledge of vowel sounds and common letter patterns, spelling must have been a complete mystery to Stephen.

On the positive side, he had learnt the rather difficult words 'friend' and 'fight' and shown that he had some idea of the spelling of 'women' and 'eye'. This evidence, plus some of his spelling that included all the letters of the word but in the wrong places, suggested that he spelt largely from recall of visual imagery words and did not know he needed to write a letter or group of letters for every sound he heard. (This was later found to be true.) His handwriting style was an additional burden that needed to be addressed.

Planning Stephen's tutoring programme

Goal setting

Goal	Time frame
1 Handwriting Goal: To develop an efficient, smooth and relatively easy writing style	In 8 weeks
2 School weekly test Goal: To know how to spell 80 per cent of the words in the weekly test at school	By the 3rd week
Goal: To memorise words using the CHIMP strategy (see Appendix 2)	By the 3rd week
3 Listening to separate sounds Goal: To be able to identify the separate sounds within a word	In 8 weeks
4 Writing the sounds in correct order Goal: To listen to the chunks of sound as he writes	In 13 weeks
Goal: To write the chunks of sound in the correct order	In 14 weeks
5 Vowel sounds Goal: To know and identify name and short vowel sounds	In 4 weeks

6 High frequency words
   Goal: To learn the five most used words each week
   Note: By the end of term 3 Stephen should have learnt 200 list words
	By the end of each week

7 Writing Goal: To reduce errors by 25 per cent	In 12 weeks
Goal: To find 80 per cent of errors in his own writing	In 24 weeks
Goal: To write in full sentences	In 24 weeks

8 Letter patterns
  Goal: To identify a range of letter
    patterns when reading
	In 12 weeks

Goal: To learn the words in groups
    according to their letter patterns
    using 'Now I can spell and read
    better too' Curriculum Standards
    Framework Level 2 (B)
	In 24 weeks

9 Rule and strategy Goal: To know how to add a suffix	In 15 weeks

Details of the programme

The time frame of the case study was ten weeks of an ongoing programme, during which several goals were addressed concurrently.

1 Handwriting

Goal: To develop an efficient, smooth and relatively easy writing style.

Action and outcome

Stephen wrote clumsily and shifted his hand for almost every letter. The author looked at the way he was holding and moving his pen, his arm and hand; how he was slanting his paper and forming his letters.

With some reluctance at first, Stephen agreed to angle the paper to the left and hold his arm much lower on the page. Writing cursively was difficult because he started some letters in the wrong place, however, he corrected this relatively easily. But his movement remained a problem as he seemed unable to flex his wrist, claiming that 'it hurt' to do so.

Evaluation

Within two weeks, Stephen no longer wrote with his arm 'over-the-top' and by the end of three months, he was still writing stiffly but more fluently and in cursive style. There was improvement and Stephen seemed a bit more relaxed. If there are no physical remedies for the stiffness in his wrist, it may be something he has to live with.

2 Weekly test at school

Goal: To know how to spell 80 per cent of the words in the weekly test at school.
Goal: To memorise words for the weekly class test, using the CHIMP strategy (see Appendix 2).

Action and outcome

Stephen usually brought the words for his weekly test to the sessions with the author, and very quickly began improving his results. The goal was to be doing the same test as the rest of the class and achieving good results.

In learning the 'CHIMP' Strategy (see Appendix 2), Stephen succeeded competently in each step, which was encouraging. By the fifth session, he had chosen to learn the word 'kaleidoscope' (a 'Champion' word from the class list) for the next session. He spelt the word correctly both forwards and backwards. During the tenth session, he spelt the word 'encyclopedia' correctly. At the time of writing Stephen was doing six of the class words in each test with some success.

Evaluation

Stephen seemed reasonably content with his progress. Since homework was something of a marathon for him, it was not always possible for him to learn all of the words. (After six months, he is being tested only on the class list and sometimes gains 10/10.)

3 Listening to separate sounds

Goal: To be able to identify the separate sounds within a word.

This goal involved Stephen:
- pronouncing words clearly, as a whole and in chunks
- understanding that every sound needs a new letter (or group of letters).

Action and outcomes

Stephen did not realise that the letters represented sounds and that each different sound group needs a different letter or chunk. He thought that every word was an independent item that you just 'had to know'.

To encourage clarity of speech, the author sometimes pretended to not catch what he said. He then repeated more clearly.

When Stephen omitted a sound or syllable in his writing the author would encourage him to say the word with her very slowly, drawing attention to the changes in his mouth and throat. Then Stephen would 'number off the bits [chunks] on [his] fingers' before writing the word again. This helped him to recognise the separate sounds in each word.

Evaluation

Stephen was more aware of separate sounds although he was not always immediately able to hear or 'feel' the separate sounds. But he now appreciated the connection between the sounds and the written letters and that made a big difference.

4 Writing the sounds in the correct order

Goal: To listen to the chunks of sound as he writes.
Goal: To write the chunks of sound in the correct order.

Action and outcome

Stephen had been relying on his inefficient visual memory of words. The habit of trying to remember the letters (by name) and spelling them out was difficult to unlearn. But with encouragement, Stephen started to listen to how the word sounded and to 'say as I go'. The first step in the CHIMP strategy (see Appendix 2) supports this learning. In tutoring sessions, when Stephen started to spell out a word, he was asked to say the word as he went.

Evaluation

There was improvement and at the time of writing Stephen was close to achieving this goal.

5 Vowel sounds

Goal: To know and identify name and short vowel sounds.

Action and outcomes

Stephen took home a chart for each set of vowels so that he could practise learning. This was reviewed in subsequent sessions through the use of testing or playing games. The author also drew Stephen's attention to vowels and their sounds in other reading and spelling activities.

Evaluation

Stephen almost knew the vowel sounds, although he sometimes wrote the wrong sound and had to be corrected, especially with the short vowel sounds, particularly 'a'. At the time of writing Stephen was close to achieving this goal.

6 High frequency words

Goal: To learn the five most used words each week.

Action and outcome

Some of these words were included in Stephen's spelling words from school. Stephen started making a 200 Most Used Words list, and used some of these to draw out his regular writing. While Stephen remembered some of the words, he did not always retain those that he had written wrongly many times.

Evaluation

At the time of writing Stephen did not know all the words thoroughly, although he did write many more words correctly. It was planned to adopt a more systematic approach of setting and testing five words each week, especially in context.

7 Writing

Goal: To reduce errors by 25 per cent.
Goal: To find 80 per cent of errors in his own writing.
Goal: To write in full sentences.

Action and outcomes

The author found that it helped Stephen's writing if the paragraph was first planned. This reduced the errors, at least in key words (providing he copied them correctly). In one session, Stephen chose the topic 'Hockey' and drew a mind map. This enabled him to write the key words correctly spelt within the paragraph. He was also asked to write up each 'branch', putting a full stop at the end of each sentence. Stephen continued practising this each week, writing at least a couple of sentences and learning the basics of punctuation. Stephen used the chart which showed the different ways that sounds can be written. This helped him to choose appropriate letters and reinforced the concept of letter patterns.

Evaluation

Stephen's 40-word piece of writing that he presented for assessment after three months of sessions with the author included six errors (2 per cent of the total). This number of errors was much lower than in his previous writing (22 per cent), although the quality of his expression was more limited in the second piece than in the first. It was decided to introduce dictation to help the process.

8 Letter patterns

Goal: To identify a range of letter patterns when reading.

Goal: To learn the words in groups according to their letter patterns using Curriculum Standards Framework Level 2 (B).

Action and outcomes

Stephen discussed the letter patterns, and words that belonged to each group of letter patterns, using his school spelling word list as a starting point. The author focused on the harder words during the sessions. At the time of writing Stephen was getting the basic words in his modified set correct in school tests, as well as most of the 'Champion' words.

Playing Snap, using cards with words to match with letter patterns seemed to help Stephen recognise the patterns quickly. He was most enthusiastic about beating the author.

Evaluation

Stephen was starting to understand and remember many of the letter patterns, especially when reading. He spelt the group words well when they were presented as a group. It remains to be seen whether he will remember them when writing and not when specifically concentrating on them.

9 Rule and strategy

Goal: To know how to add a suffix.

Action and outcome

The author showed Stephen the rule to follow when adding suffixes (two consonants after the short vowel sound in the word and only one consonant after a name vowel sound). Stephen revised this rule many times during the course of the sessions.

Stephen practised reading and spelling words during games such as Noughts and Crosses and Battleships. When tested with nonsense words, Stephen was correct on four out of five 'words', was able to repeat the rule and then self-correct the one error.

Evaluation

Stephen learnt this strategy very quickly and was starting to develop the concept of base word, prefix and suffix.

South Australian Spelling Test

Stephen scored 31 in the South Australian Spelling Test (Westwood, 1999), which was equivalent to other students aged 8.6 years. While this is three years lower than his age, it indicates an increase of one year level in three months. When asked why he wrote 'chip' instead of 'chop' he replied, 'Oops. I didn't listen'. This comment shows real progress.

Spelling in context of writing

This is a typed version of a passage of Stephen's writing. The word 'jamboree' was supplied. Stephen had only ten minutes to complete this and proof-read. The deletions and added full stops were made in the editing process.

> *On Januyey 5th for 12 days and it was fun and all these bans [bands] came. We went to homebouse [Homebush], wonerland into the city. The Jamboree had a water siled it was fun and a b,m.x track and we slept in tins [tents]. We had to, cook all meles.*

Comments on progress

Although it contains many errors, this passage is translatable and shows application of learning, such as 'meles' for 'meals' – the wrong but logical letter pattern. The passage is not as rich in construction and vocabulary as his initial spelling in context assessment. Since he is more conscious of spelling now, Stephen may be limiting his words to those he has a better chance of getting right. This will be addressed in future by setting some tasks in which he concentrates on the content and edits after, rather than trying to do both at once. The author believes, in time, he will be able to do both.

Stephen tended to give monosyllabic answers even to open questions, using only key words. But, because his message was conveyed adequately, the author noticed it only when Stephen read aloud something he had written in half-formed sentences and it sounded just as he talked. One way to encourage him to talk more, was to ask, 'What did you do just before you came? And just before that? And just before that?'. This allowed him to use his visual strength and elicited much fuller replies.

Including maths and reading practice in Stephen's programme may have increased the time needed to achieve all spelling goals but, at the time of writing he was continuing to improve, nevertheless. He is happier in terms of his success at school and also the results of his assessment. He is very proud of some of the difficult words he is memorising. As his mother said, 'I think the light is turning on.' It will be important to consolidate his current learning and continue developing the goals as indicated in planning.

Notes

1 The Department for Education and Employment in the UK recognises the term 'dyslexia', which is defined thus: 'Dyslexia is a combination of abilities and difficulties which affect the learning process in reading, spelling, writing and sometimes numeracy. Dyslexic people frequently have weaknesses in short-term memory, sequencing and processing information – skills everyone needs to learn effectively in a busy classroom. What may start as a learning difference quickly becomes a learning difficulty if dyslexia goes unrecognised and the teaching is appropriate.' The British Dyslexic Association and the Department of Education and Employment, *Achieving Dyslexic Friendly Schools*, London: Education Authority.

2 Spelling improvement can be brought about in poor spellers if proper instruction is carried out systematically over a long period of time, and the spelling instruction is tailored to match the development level of a student's word knowledge. Moats, L. C. (1995), *Spelling: Development, Disability and Instruction*, Baltimore, MD: York Press.

3 Examples are the Spalding method, THRASS and Roberts, J. (2000), *Now I Can Spell and Read Better, Too*, Melbourne: Learning Pathways.

4 Imagery training in a Year 3 research indicated that the best results were gained by children who engaged in strategy training plus whole language. Butyniec-Thomas, J. and Woloshyn, V. E. (1997), 'The effects of explicit strategy and whole language instruction on students' spelling ability', *Journal of Experimental Education*, 65, 4, 293–302.

5 While there is some merit in learning the individual words in a particular list, the real value comes from learning how to learn words. Westwood, P. (1999), *Spelling: Approaches to Teaching and Assessment*, Melbourne: ACER Press.

6 Passy, J. (1990) *Cued Articulation*, Melbourne: ACER Press.

7 Ibid.

8 One source of dictation is Roberts, J. (2000), *Now I Can Spell and Read Better, Too*, Melbourne: Learning Pathways.

Spelling Error Analysis Record

Name .... Age .... Year .... Date ....

Misspelt words Student's spelling (+ correct spelling)	Word categories		Types of errors				More severe problems, if frequent errors here	
	High frequency word 135 *or R = Relatively,* *for age*	Irregular or difficult spelling *I = Irregular* *D = Difficult,* *relative to age*	Logical phonetic spelling	Incorrect choice *Vowel, Consonant,* *Letter pattern,* *Homophone*	Incorrect use of spelling rule or convention	Morphemic or etymological errors	Wrong order, Omission, Addition, Substitution, Limited approximation	Miscellaneous, e.g. *No attempt, Limited output, Crossing out, Copying problems*

Name .... Date ....

Note relevant factors possibly contributing to errors

Major known:
e.g. English as second language, specific disability

....

Physical
e.g. Hearing, speech, vision, handwriting, posture

....

Intellectual, cognitive
e.g. Memory: auditory and visual, processing, attention, strategies, reading

....

Emotional
e.g. Anxiety, trauma, relationships

....

Environmental
e.g. Lighting, heat, cold, position in room, trauma, relationships

....

Note strengths shown and other beneficial factors

Student knowledge of content, strategies. Attitude

....

Additional help available

....

Other

....

The CHIMP strategy

The word CHIMP is an acronym for the four steps in the process:

1 **CH**unk
2 **I**nvestigate
3 **M**emory screen
4 **P**ractise!

Applying the strategy to the word 'happiness'

1 Chunk

- Break the word into chunks (of sound) and count the chunks:
  happiness = 3
- Write the word in separate chunks:
  happ   in   ess
  or
  hap   pin   ness

2 Investigate

In any order:

- Explore the meaning and others in the family, for example happy, happily.
- Look and listen to the spelling. Short vowels 'a', 'i'; half-sound (or schwa) vowel 'e'; double ss.
- Note anything else, for example the word 'pin'.
- Decide on the trickiest part of the word. How will you remember it? Highlight it.

3 Memory screen

- Close your eyes and imagine a big screen. Look up at it.
- Put the chunks of the word on the screen.
- Read (that is spell) the word forwards and backwards

4 Practise!

Write the word at least three times, saying the chunks aloud, and synchronising hand and voice.

Strategy to write an unknown word

Students can use this three-step process for selected words. Knowledge of the CHIMP strategy enhances the effectiveness of this one.

For example, imagine John wants to write the word 'aerodynamic' and does not know how to spell it. He takes the following steps.

1 Search

John looks up behind closed eyes and says, 'Where have I seen this word before?' Often, students will magically 'find' the word they want – they are able to recall it from some experience – and can reproduce it perfectly. Sometimes the student will remember that the word is handy in a list or text. If not, they can move on to the next step.

2 Chunk and think

John says the word in chunks, using fingers as in the CHIMP strategy (aerodynamic = five chunks). He then thinks for a moment about the spelling in each chunk. That is, 'How will I spell 'air'? o? di? nam? ic?' He can write it the best way he can or refer to Different ways to spell a sound (see Appendix 6) where he may remember that the 'aer' letter pattern is at the beginning.

3 Write and check

John writes the word, saying it as he writes. Then he looks at it and adjusts the spelling if he thinks his version is not quite right. If he is still having difficulties, he needs to know he can go for help.

135 most used words

A
about
after
all
am
an
and
are
as
at
away

B
baby
back
ball
be
because
bed
been
before
big
boy
but
by

C
called
came
can
children
Christmas
come
could ✗

D
dad
day
did
do
dog
doing
down

E
egg

F
first
for
friend
from

G
get
girl
go
going
good

H
had
has
have
he
her
here
him
his
home
house

I
I
if
in
into
is
it

J
just

L
like
liked
little
look

M
made
make
me
more
mum
my
much
must

N
new
no
not
now

O
of
off

old
on
one
only
or
other
our
out
outside
over

P
play
played
put

R
ran
right ✗

S
said
saw
school
see
she
so
some

T
that
the
their ✗
them
then
there ✗

they
this
time
to
took
two

U
up

V
very

W
want
was
we
well
went
were
what
when
where
which
who
will
with
would

Y
you
yours

Z
zebra
zoo

Adapted from Westwood, (1999), *Spelling: Approaches to Teaching and Assessment*, ACER Press, Melbourne

330 most frequently used words

A 28.2.05

about
actually —
after
afternoon
again
against
allowed (to) —
almost
although —
annually —
another
answered —
anything
apparently —
April
arc (circular) —
aren't
argue
argument
around
asked
ate
athlete
August —
awful —

B 7/3/05

babies
beautiful
because
before
beginning —
being
believe —
benefit —

between
bicycle —
bought —
break
brief —
brought
built
bury —
busy
buy

C

cannot
can't
carries —
caught —
celery —
certain
children
Christmas 14.3.05
climbed
clothes
colour
committee
could
couldn't
country
course
cousin
cricket

D

daughter —
deceive
December
definitely

description
different
difficult
disappearance
disappointed
disguise
does
doesn't
done
double
during

25.4.05

E

each
early
Easter
eating
eighth
either
else
enemy
enough
escape
everywhere
exaggerate
eyes

F

fasten
fault
February
few
fight
finally
foreign
forgotten

forty
friendly
frightened

G

generally
give
goal
goes
goodbye
government
great
grew
guessed
guilty

H

half
happened
happily
have
haven't
head
heard
heavy
here
holiday
hour
hungry
hurriedly
husband
hygiene

I

ice-cream
I'd *(I would)*

I'll *(I will)*
I'm *(I am)*
independent
indicate
instead
interesting
interrupt
it's *(it is)*
its *(something*
  belongs to it)
I've *(I have)*

J

January
judgement
jumper
June
July
justice

K

keep
kept
kick
kitchen
knew
knife
knight
knives
know

L

ladies
language
last
laugh

leisure
lettuce
light
listen
little
loose
lose
lost
love

M
magazine
majority
many
marriage
meant
medicine
might
Miss
Monday
money
more
Mr
Mrs
Ms
myself

N
necessary
neighbour
neither
never
niece
nineteen
ninth
none
nothing
November

O
occasionally

occurred
October
often
once
one
onion
opposite
orchestra
other

P
parallel
parents
party
passed
peaceful
peculiar
people
perfectly
permanent
piano
picnic
piece (of)
pleasant
possession
potato
potatoes
prefer
pretty
public

Q
queen
quickly
quietly
quite

R
raise
rapid
received
repetition

right
　(side/correct)

S
safety
said
sandwich
Saturday
school
self
sense
separate
September
sew *(material)*
shall
shoes
should
shouldn't
silence
since
sincerely
sister
soldier
some
something
statue
straight
studying
success
sufficient
sugar
surprise

T
taught
tear
tell
thank
that's
their *(house)*
there *(is, will)*
these

they
they'll
think
thirteen
though
thought
threw
throw
Thursday
tired
together
told
tomorrow
too
tried
trying
Tuesday
twelve (12)
twenty (20)
two (2)

U
until
unusual
upon
used to

V
very

W
walked
wanted
war
warm
was
washed
wasn't
water
Wednesday
we'll
were

weren't
what
when
where
which
while
white
who
whom
who's
　(who is)
whose
　(whose bag?)
why
woman *(one)*
women
　(plural)
won't
work
worry
worst
would
wouldn't
write
writing

X
xylophone

Y
yacht
yellow
yesterday
your
yours

Z
zebra
zoo

Different ways to spell a sound

Consonant sounds

C **K** **cat** **kill** **back** gekko echo	**F** **fun** **puff** elephant laugh	**G** **go** **egg** ghost	**J** **jump giraffe** fudge
M **man** **swimmer** bomb	**N** **nut** **running** knot gnome	**Q** **queen** choir	**R** **run** **ferry** writing rhythm
S and Z **sun** **dress face** **was** xylophone precious champagne	**SH** **shed** **station** tension passion	**T** **top** **sitting** **picked**	**W** **watch** language
X **box** **sticks**			

Vowel sounds

AY **day** **name rain** grey eight vein	**AR** **car** **fast** calm	**AIR** **hair** **share bear** there their canary they're	**E** **bed** **dead** **any** said
EE **tree** **sea** **happy she** **these** chief receive anemone	**ER** **her** **bird** **fur** word early journey were	**I** **igloo pyramid** busy women build choir	**I** **time** **find** **tie** **fly** **high** dye buy height
O **dog** **was** shoulder	**O** **hose** **goat** **go** **show toe**	**U** **umbrella zebra** **come** **mother** doctor country	**U** **due** **few** beautiful
OO **moon blue** **do** **grew**	**OO** **book put** should woman	**OU** **house cow** **flour** bough	**OR** **fork** **more paw** four caution war walk bought

Demon words

A

ache
actually
afraid
again
against
allowed
all right
although
always
angry
animals
annually
another
answered
any
argument
around
asked
asks
athlete
awful

B

babies
beautiful
because
before
beginning
believe
benefit
bicycle
bought
break
breath *(noun)*

breathe *(verb)*
brief
brought
built
bureaucracy
burglar
buried
bury
busily
business
busy
buy

C

can't
carrying
catastrophe
caught
celery
certain
children
choose
Christmas
climb/ed
clothes
colour
come
coming
committee
conscious
could have
could've *(could have)*
country
course
cousin

D

daughter
dear
deceive
definitely
description
diarrhoea
didn't
different
difficult
disappearance
disappointed
disguised
doctor
does
doesn't
done
double
dropped

E

early
Easter
eighth
either
elephant
else
enemy
enough
enthusiasm
escape
everywhere
exaggerate
exhibition

F

families
family
fasten
fault
February
fell
felt
finally
first
for
foreign
forgotten
forty
friendly
friends
frightened

G

goodbye
government
guessed
guilty

H

half
happened
happily
heard
here
here's
holiday
hospital
hour
hungry
hurriedly
husband
hygienic

I

I'd/I'll/I'm
independent

indicate
instead
integration
interesting
interrupt
its *(e.g. its tail)*
it's *(= it is)*

J

judge
judgement
just
justice

K

kinaesthetic
kitchen
knew
knife/knives
knot
know

L

ladies
language
leisure
lettuce
let's *(let us)*
lettuce
loose *(not tight,
    not controlled)*
lose

M

magazine
majority
maroon *(colour)*
marriage
meant
medicine
minute
mischievous
money
mortgage

N

name
naming
necessary
neighbour
neither
niece
ninety
ninth
none

O

occasionally
occurred
often
once
onion
opposite
orchestra

P

parallel
passed
peaceful
people
perfectly
permanent
piano
picnic
picture
piece *(of something)*
pleasant
possession
potato/potatoes
practice *(noun—the thing
    [practice] you do)*
practise *(verb—doing it: I
    practise every day)*
prefer
preference
pretty/prettiest
principal *(main)*

principle *(the central idea, the moral)*
probably
pumpkin
pyjamas

Q
quiet *(peaceful)*
quietly
quite *(a fair bit, moderately)*

R
raise
rapidly
read
ready
receive
received
repetition
rotten

S
safety
said
sandwich
Saturday
says
scheme
school
sense
separate
shining
shoes
silence
since
sincerely

soldier
statue
straight
studying
success
sufficient
sugar
surprise
swimming

T
taught
tear
temperature
than *(e.g. taller than me)*
that's *(that is)*
there *(position)*
their *(their things)*
there's *(there is)*
they
they're
though
thought
through
tired
together
too *(We went, too. It is too long)*
tough
travelled
trouble
truly
Tuesday
twelve

U
until

unusual
used
usually

V
valuable
vegetables
very
view

W
wanted
wear *(clothes)*
weather
Wednesday
week
were *(We were)*
where *(? place)*
whether *(if)*
which *(which one?)*
who's *(Who is coming?)*
whose *(whose bag?)*
woman
women
won't
worst
would
writing
wrote

X
xylophone

Y
yacht
yours

Other personal demons

Spelling Rules and Ways to Remember

There are spelling rules, even though the rules are sometimes broken, and mnemonic cues (memory tricks) worth knowing. Introduce them, not as 'They who must be obeyed' but as 'Handy hints to make spelling easier'.

Vowels

- A vowel in every chunk
  There is at least one vowel in every chunk [assuming 'y' is also a vowel],
  e.g. In   b / a / g   hap / py   h / ou / se   com / put / er
  Exceptions: words such as rhythm, spasm, chasm

- Ugh! The schwa sound you hardly hear
  We hardly hear the 'schwa' vowel, eg between, apparently, profit, attain
  It sometimes helps to think of other words in the meaning family, e.g. happiness, necessity

- Short vowel sounds
  When you hear a short vowel sound, write the letter that says that sound, e.g. cat, leg, tin, dog, fun, dad, run
  Some useful exceptions:
  – 'a' says Short Vowel 'o' in: was, want, what; a says e in any, many;
  – 'a' says Short Vowel 'u' only at the very end of a word, never in the middle,
  e.g. tuna, Lisa, zebra

- Long/Name Vowel sounds (C V C E)
  'e' on the end helps the vowel say its name (usually), e.g. name, tune, time, hope, face, these

Adding a suffix that starts with a vowel, e.g. ing, ed, er, est

- Adding the suffix to a word with a short vowel chunk
  To add on a suffix, e.g. ing, ed, er or 'y', to a word or chunk with a Short Vowel sound, you usually need two consonants. If there is only one, you will need to double, e.g. run-running, hop-hopped, sit-sitting, fun-funny
  But, you don't need to double if:
  – there are already two consonants: e.g. send / ing   stand / ing
  – when you add to an unstressed vowel chunks that end in 't', 'l' or 'p',
  e.g. credit-credited, benefit-benefiting, market-marketed, profit-profiting, parallel-paralleled, gossip-gossiped

- Adding the suffix to a word with a Name (Long) Vowel chunk
  To add on (ed, ing, er, y) to a word or chunk with a Name/Long vowel sound that ends with 'e', drop the 'e', then add the suffix. There will be just one consonant before the suffix, e.g. tape-taping, hope-hoped
  Exceptions: After a soft 'g' and 'o', when adding 'able', leave the 'e' to keep the 'g' or 'c' soft sound, e.g. trace/able   manage/able   service/able

- Adding the suffix to a word with a letter pattern
  After Letter Pattern chunks, as in park and cool, just add the ending,
  e.g. read-reading   fair-fairy   park-parked
  NOTE: To add a suffix that starts with a consonant, e.g. ment, ful
  Usually, just add the ending, e.g. hopeful, appointment
  For a word ending with a 'y', change the 'y' to 'i' then add the ending,
  e.g. happy-happiness, pretty-prettiest

Adding a prefix, e.g. re, un

- You just write the prefix and add on the word, e.g. re + submit = resubmit,
  un + necessary = unnecessary, dis + appointment = disappointment,
  dis + loyal + dis/loyal.
  ★ Sometimes this means that two of the same letters are side by side, e.g. dissatisfied, misspent, unnecessary. When these are vowels, we can separate them with a hyphen (although this is often omitted in current publications): e.g. re-enter, co-operation or cooperation

Letter pattern

- 'When two vowels go walking, the first one does the talking.' In this letter pattern the first one says the sound, e.g. train   day   meat   boat   flow

- ie or ei
  It's 'i' before 'e', but swap after a 'c', when the sound is 'ee', e.g. achieve, believe, grief, brief, siege and receive, conceive, deceit
  The four exceptions: The weird sheik seized the protein weir.

Practice or Practise?

- PRACTICE is a noun – the something you do: e.g. I must go and do my practice;
- PRACTISE is a verb – an action word in the sentence: e.g. Go and practise that technique.
  Note: In American spelling, the word is written with a 'c' for both noun and verb.

Annotated bibliography

Andrew, M. (1997) *Reading and Spelling Made Simple*, ACER, and Gamlen Press, Melbourne.
A guide to helping students with learning difficulties to learn letter patterns.

Edwards, P. (1981) *Primary Education*, Nelson, Melbourne.
Unfortunately this text is currently out of print but worth using if you can find a copy.

Nicholson, T. (1999) *At the Cutting Edge: Read and Spell for Success*, NZER, New Zealand.
Full of interesting research information on what works including detailed information about phonemic awareness.

Roberts, J. (2000) *Now I Can Spell and Read Better, Too*, Learning Pathways, Melbourne.
A structured programme for students from Prep to Year 9, including assessment, games and activities, and dictation.

Schonell F. and Wise, P. (1993) *Essentials in Teaching and Testing Spelling* (2nd edn), NFER, Nelson, Melbourne.
Explains the importance of spelling. Games and activities for consolidation, vocabulary and dictionary work.

Spalding, R. B. (1990) *The Writing Road to Reading*, William Morrow, New York.
A structured spelling programme suitable for all ages.

Westwood, P. (1999) *Spelling: Approaches to Teaching and Assessment*, ACER Press, Melbourne.
Clearly written description of the acquisition of spelling skills, suggestions for implementing teaching and assessment details. Includes the South Australian Spelling Test.

Index

Index